EXPLORE

EXPERIMENT

AND DISCOVER

SCIENCE

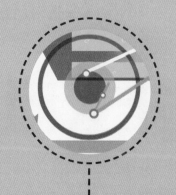

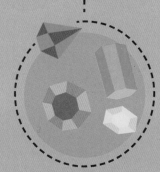

This edition published by Parragon Books Ltd in 2016 and distributed by
Parragon Inc.
440 Park Avenue South, 13th Floor
New York, NY 10016
www.parragon.com

Written by Anna Claybourne
Illustrated by Susanna Rumiz, Genie Espinosa
Consultant: Jack Challoner

ISBN 978-1-4748-2980-9

Printed in China

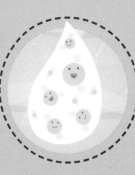

Discovery KIDS™

FACTIVITY™

EXPLORE
EXPERIMENT
AND DISCOVER
SCIENCE

PaRragon

Bath • New York • Cologne • Melbourne • Delhi
Hong Kong • Shenzhen • Singapore • Amsterdam

Contents

You'll find the puzzle answers at the back of the book.

Check out the glossary for any special science words.

So, what is science?

Science is amazing! It's how we find out about almost everything. Scientists are always asking questions—they want to understand the world and how and why stuff happens!

Here are some of the things that scientists do.

QUESTION

What are stars actually made of?

What makes a soda fizzy?

How do you make shadows?

Why do birds sing?

OBSERVE

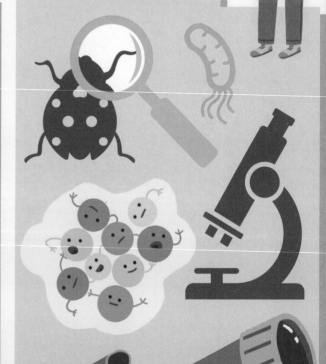

Taking a closer look can help!

MEASURE

How many? How hot, cold, big, small? What changed, and when?

CLASSIFY

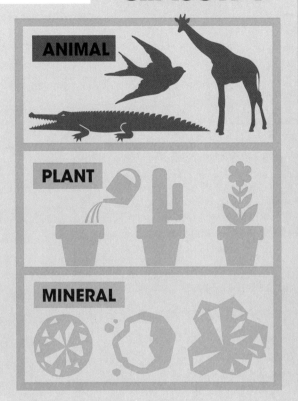

ANIMAL

PLANT

MINERAL

EXPERIMENT

Will it fly? Is it strong? Will it change color?

EXPLAIN

Figure out why things happen, and share your knowledge.

Let's experiment!

Many scientists find the answers to their questions by doing experiments. They carefully test their ideas to figure out if they are correct—or if it's time for a rethink!

All experiments have some steps in common—this is called the scientific method.

From studying tiny insects to making new medicines, experiments help scientists to find the answers.

1 Observe, measure, and collect information.

6 Start again with a new theory!

2 Ask a question or come up with a THEORY about WHY or HOW what you have seen happens.

5 Do your results prove that your theory is right?

3 Figure out an experiment to test your theory. Do the experiment!

4 Record your results.

Scientists look out for changes when they experiment. Can you find eight changes between these two laboratory pictures?

When you mix things up, sometimes you get a big reaction!

BEFORE

The science of living things is called Biology.

AFTER

Some experiments look at how things react together. This branch of science is called Chemistry.

Other experiments look at forces and how and why things move. This type of science is called Physics.

9

Science and inventions

Science isn't just about theories—it also provides the big ideas behind all kinds of great inventions, from light bulbs to space rockets. Inventors find practical uses for scientific discoveries.

The world is full of bright ideas—like light bulbs!

Have you ever seen steam coming out of a teakettle?

The Ancient Greeks used steam to power the aeolipile—the world's first steam engine.

More than a thousand years later, scientists and engineers figured out how to harness steam power.

This useful power source led to inventions such as steam trains!

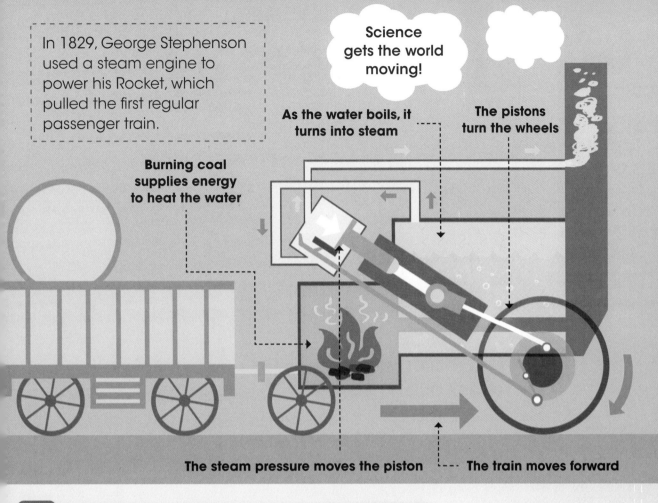

In 1829, George Stephenson used a steam engine to power his Rocket, which pulled the first regular passenger train.

Science gets the world moving!

As the water boils, it turns into steam

The pistons turn the wheels

Burning coal supplies energy to heat the water

The steam pressure moves the piston

The train moves forward

What will you invent? Imagine and draw a car, plane, train, boat, or spaceship of the future!

What is energy?

Energy makes things happen! It's the power behind everything, and you use it every time you do something. Energy never gets used up; it just changes from one type to another.

Follow the routes to discover some of the different types of energy.

MOVEMENT

Phew! All this jumping is making me super hot!

It takes energy to get things moving or to stop them.

E N E

START

START

START

LIGHT

Light is a form of energy that we can see. It's always moving and can't be stored.

Now I can see what you mean about energy!

Electrical energy powers everything from light bulbs to computers.

ELECTRICAL

THERMAL

BRRR

We call the energy that comes from hot things "thermal energy."

Chemical energy can come from food that you have digested.

Energy can be stored as chemical energy. Food contains chemical energy—so do batteries and firewood.

START

START

RGY

START

CHEMICAL

Sound energy needs something to travel through. The sound of this trumpet travels through the air.

SOUND

Light and shade

Light is a type of energy that we can see. It comes from light sources, such as light bulbs or the Sun. It shines out in lots of straight lines called light rays or beams.

We see things around us even if they don't give out light. This is because light bounces off them and into our eyes.

Light rays →

Light from the Sun takes more than eight minutes to reach Earth.

Light travels very fast, but the Sun is about 91 million miles away!

Shadow

Shadows are caused where something blocks the light.

LIGHT RAYS

Light rays are made of many waves of light energy. The separate waves are too small to see—you just see the light shining.

 Make these animal shadows with your hands! This works best in a dark room with just one light shining onto a plain wall.

DUCK

Light rays can't bend around things, so this leaves a dark area of shadow where the light can't reach.

RABBIT

Light rays can zoom through air, water, or even empty space.

DOG

Tricks of the light

Remember how light usually travels in straight lines? Well, light can also do clever tricks like bouncing off of shiny surfaces—or even bending as it moves!

Shiny mirrors bounce light back very evenly to create reflections.

When light hits a shiny surface like a mirror, it bounces back. This bouncing of light is called **reflection**.

Your reflection is shown in reverse, so your left hand becomes your right in a mirror.

Rough surfaces bounce light in lots of different directions. That's why you can't see a reflection of yourself on a wall.

Alice Through the Looking Glass

When you look at yourself in a mirror, what you are really seeing is reflected light.

 Reflections reverse writing, too. Hold this page up to a mirror to read the title of this book!

In a curved mirror, light bounces off at strange angles, creating funny, uneven reflections!

Ha ha! I've been stretched.

Draw a wobbly reflection of yourself in this curved mirror!

EXPERIMENT ZONE

You will need:
- A clear glass
- A straw
- Water

Try this experiment to see light bend when it moves through water.

As well as bouncing, light can bend when it moves from one see-through substance into another.

❶

Put a straw into a glass, and look through the glass at the straw. Does it look straight? Now fill the glass with water and look again.

❷

What's changed? The straw looks broken because light bends as it moves between water, glass, and air. This bending is called refraction.

Look closer

Time to zoom in! Bending light through curved pieces of glass called lenses can make things look BIGGER. Scientists use lenses in telescopes and microscopes to take a closer look at the world.

TELESCOPE

A simple telescope has two lenses inside a tube. Around 400 years ago, Italian scientist Galileo built a telescope to study the night sky.

Zooming in let Galileo see that the planet Jupiter had several moons.

He could also see and draw the craters on Earth's Moon.

The lenses in a telescope collect and bend lots of light from distant objects to make them look bigger.

MICROSCOPE

The microscope was invented in the 1590s by Hans and Zacharius Jansen.

Microscopes bend light in a similar way to telescopes, so that you can zoom in on very small objects.

Animal cells

Microscopes were improved and made popular by the scientist Robert Hooke.

Microscopic animals

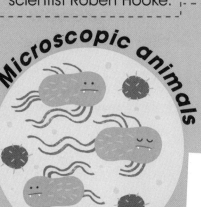

Looking through a microscope, Hooke drew the tiny things he saw.

Connect the dots to see one of the tiny animals Hooke saw through his microscope. What kind of creature was it?

Plant cells

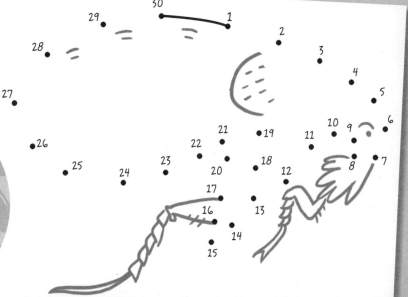

What are colors?

Light is a mix of all the colors of the rainbow! When light strikes an object, some colors are absorbed and some bounce off. A green T-shirt absorbs all the colors except green, which bounces off.

We know that light contains many different colors, thanks to an experiment by the scientist Isaac Newton in 1666.

COLOR SPECTRUM

VIOLET

INDIGO

BLUE

GREEN

YELLOW

ORANGE

RED

Newton shone sunlight through a glass block called a prism. It split out into a display of different colors, which he called a spectrum.

Glass prism - - - - - - - - - - - →

Light bends (refracts) when it passes through the glass prism. Some colors bend more than others, making them separate out.

X-rays and other rays

There are several types of wave similar to light, but they are outside the spectrum we can see. These waves are invisible but can be very useful and have led to some amazing inventions.

Radio waves are another type of invisible energy wave. They are used to send signals long distances, which can then be turned into sounds at the other end!

One of the most useful types of invisible energy wave was discovered by Wilhelm Roentgen in 1895. He called the mysterious new waves "X-rays!"

X-rays help doctors to see broken bones.

Color in the areas marked with a dot black to reveal the other side of the X-ray.

Roentgen experimented by shining X-rays through objects. He found that he could use them to make pictures of the bones inside our bodies.

X-rays can pass through soft things like our skin and organs, but they are absorbed by hard things like bones.

Electricity

Switch on and power up! Electricity is a type of energy, and we use it to make all kinds of things work, from light bulbs to laptops. When electricity flows, it can give us light, heat, and power!

The type of electricity that moves is called current electricity!

A battery contains chemical energy, which can be turned into electrical energy.

Battery

ELECTRIC CIRCUIT

Copper and other metals allow electricity to move through them. These materials are called **conductors**.

Electricity can only flow when it has an unbroken path to travel through. This path is called a circuit.

A switch can break the circuit to stop electricity from flowing.

Switch

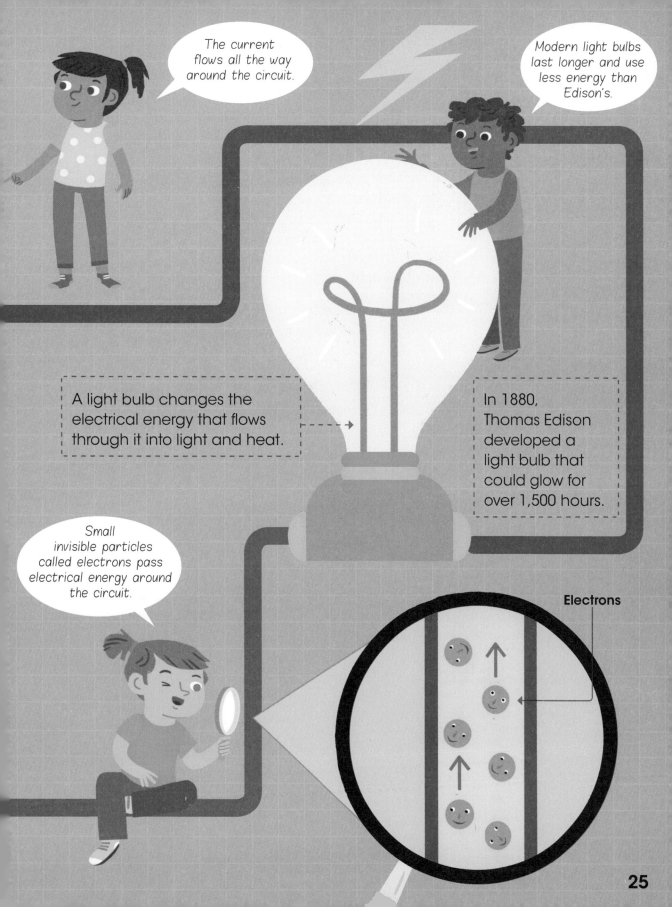

Static electricity

You might think that static electricity sounds a little dull, like it doesn't do much? Wrong! This is the kind of electricity that quietly builds up before flashing across the sky as lightning!

Static charge builds up in the clouds during a thunderstorm.

Sometimes I get an electric shock when I pick up my sweater.

That's because the static charge that has built up on its surface suddenly flows into you.

This huge negative charge sometimes jumps across to other clouds, tall buildings, trees, or the ground.

A lightning bolt is a giant static electric spark jumping between the clouds and the ground.

EXPERIMENT ZONE

 Try this totally safe, but fun, experiment to feel static electricity in action!

You will need:

- A balloon full of air
- A woolly jumper
- Torn-up pieces of tissue paper

3

Put the tissue paper pieces on a table, then rub the balloon again. Does it attract them?

Static electricity can attract your hair and make it stick to the balloon, too!

1

Rub the balloon against your sweater. The balloon now has a charge of electricity that cannot flow anywhere.

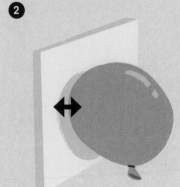

2

Place the balloon against a wall. Does it stick? The static charge should make the balloon and wall attract each other.

Make some noise!

Now hear this! Sound is caused by movements in the air called vibrations. These travel through the air as sound waves, which are then picked up by our ears.

The louder you play, the more sound energy you create!

When the guitarist plays, the strings vibrate, quickly moving backward and forward.

The moving strings push the air around them and make it vibrate, too.

The faster the strings vibrate, the higher the sound they make.

Sound energy spreads out through the air as sound waves.

When the sound waves hit our eardrums, we hear the noise that has been made.

EXPERIMENT ZONE

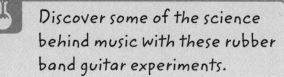

Discover some of the science behind music with these rubber band guitar experiments.

You will need:

- Thick, medium, and thin rubber bands
- An empty tissue box
- A wooden spoon

1 Stretch a thick rubber band lengthwise over an empty tissue box, and slide a wooden spoon under it. Pluck the rubber band, and listen to the sound it makes.

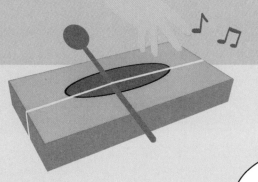

2 Now move the wooden spoon down a little, and pluck it again. Does it sound different? You should find that it has a lower sound.

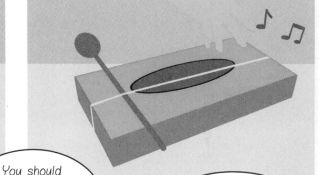

3 Now add a medium and a thin rubber band. Pluck each one and listen to the sounds they make.

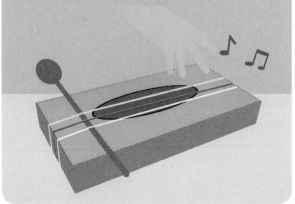

Bouncing sound

Have you ever heard an **echo**, echo, echo?
When sound waves bounce back from hard
surfaces, they create echoes.

If sound hits a hard surface, it can reflect off of it, the way light reflects from a mirror. You hear the reflected sound as an echo.

HEY

HEY

HEY

HEY

Dolphins use echoes to find their way or to hunt prey in dark water. This is called **echolocation**—bats flying at night use it, too!

Dolphins make a clicking sound.

Sound moves through the air at a speed of roughly 761 miles per hour. It can travel a mile in about five seconds.

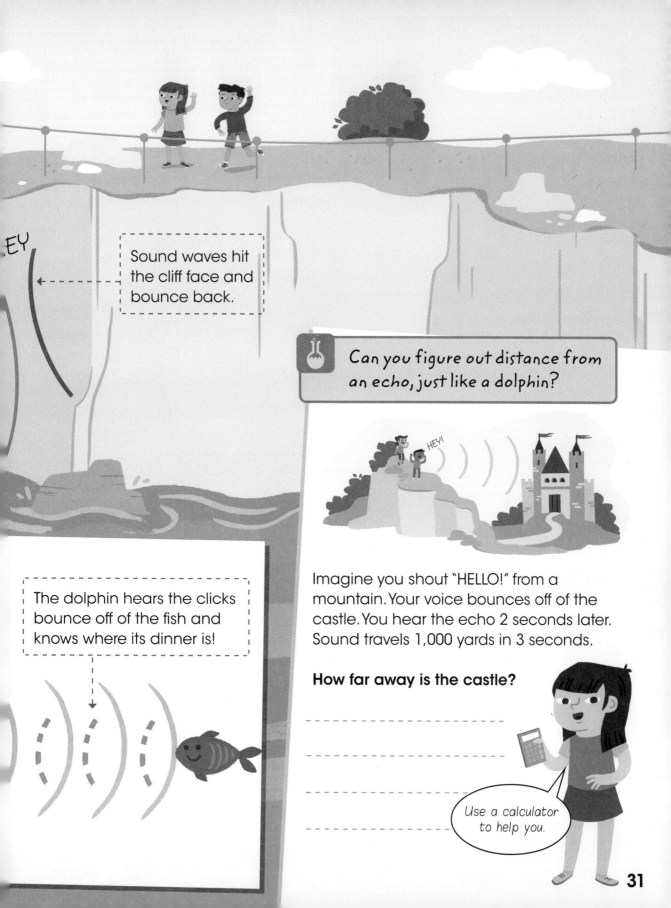

EY

Sound waves hit the cliff face and bounce back.

Can you figure out distance from an echo, just like a dolphin?

HEY!

The dolphin hears the clicks bounce off of the fish and knows where its dinner is!

Imagine you shout "HELLO!" from a mountain. Your voice bounces off of the castle. You hear the echo 2 seconds later. Sound travels 1,000 yards in 3 seconds.

How far away is the castle?

Use a calculator to help you.

Call me!

Energy can change into many different forms. Many inventions use energy changes, including the telephone. From the first telephone to modern smartphones, energy keeps us connected!

So, as I was saying, your phone just turns those signals back into sound waves!

Cell phones turn the sound energy from our voices into electrical energy and then send it as radio signals to another phone.

The first phone call EVER was made by inventor Alexander Graham Bell in 1876 on the Bell telephone he invented.

Sound waves went in through the mouthpiece and were turned into electrical signals.

Electrical signals traveled down the phone lines, which connected both ends of the telephone.

Sound energy in

Electrical energy

Can you hear me?

THE BELL TELEPHONE

EXPERIMENT ZONE

 Make your own telephone to send sound energy along a string!

You will need:
- Two plastic cups
- Three yards of string
- A friend to call!

❶

Make a small hole in the center of each cup base.

❷

Thread one end of the string through one cup, tying the knot on the inside.

Sound energy from your voice vibrates along the string and is turned back into sound at the other end.

❸

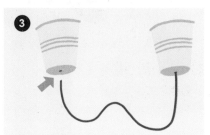

Measure three yards of string, and join the string to the other cup.

❹

Give your friend one end and ask her to put it to her ear. Then go into another room, pull the string tight, and speak into your cup.

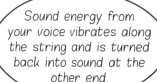

The receiver reversed the changes to create sound waves again!

Loud and ... um ... a little muffled!

Sound energy out

Energy for life

We put food into our bodies and fuel into cars. Chemical energy is stored in the materials that food and fuel are made of.

This may look like a mild-mannered banana, but under that skin, this food is really a powerhouse of chemical energy!

SUPER ENERGY!

Powering up!

I was just hungry. I had no idea I was eating super-powerful chemical energy!

Chemical energy

Our bodies use chemical energy to live—and to MOVE!

All this drumming is making me hungry!

Sound energy

Movement energy

When we move, we use up this energy. The more we move, the more food we need to eat.

The chemical energy in food is measured in calories. Which activities burn up the most energy? Match the activities to the calories they use.

 Slice of bread =100 calories

 **1** Soccer

A
450 calories per hour

 **2** Sleeping

B
600 calories per hour

 **3** Dancing

C
50 calories per hour

 **4** Cycling

D
550 calories per hour

 **5** Swimming

E
400 calories per hour

Hot and cold

What makes one drink hot and another cold? The answer is thermal energy! Temperature is dependent on how much thermal energy there is in a substance. More energy means more heat!

This milk shake is just the thing to cool me down.

COLD STRAWBERRY MILK SHAKE

HOT CHOCOLATE

Liquids are made up of tiny particles that move around.

The warmer something is, the faster its particles jiggle and move around.

When a substance is cooler, its particles move more slowly.

EXPERIMENT ZONE

You will need:

- Two see-through bowls
- Hot tap water (not too hot to touch)
- Cold tap water
- Liquid food coloring

Try this experiment to discover how thermal energy makes particles really move!

The faster the particles in the water move, the faster the color spreads.

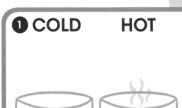

① COLD ⠀ HOT

Half-fill one bowl with cold water and the other with hot water.

② COLD ⠀ HOT

Drop one drop of food coloring into each bowl, and watch what happens.

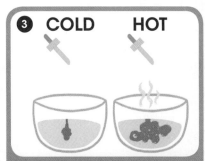

③ COLD ⠀ HOT

How fast does the food coloring spread out? You should see it spread out faster in the hot water.

When a hot object is next to a cooler object, it transfers some of its thermal energy to it.

That's why you can warm up your feet on a hot-water bottle!

Thermal energy feels nice and toasty!

THERMAL ENERGY

Heating up

When things heat up, they usually get bigger, and when they cool down, they get smaller again. As particles get hotter, they move faster and push farther away from each other, which means they take up more room.

When the liquid gets colder, it contracts (gets smaller) and moves back down the tube.

A thermometer has liquid inside. As the liquid warms up, it **expands** (gets bigger), pushing it farther up the tube to show a higher temperature.

Temperature is measured in degrees Fahrenheit.

212°

212°

32°

32°

212° Fahrenheit is the temperature at which water boils.

32° Fahrenheit is the temperature at which water freezes.

EXPERIMENT ZONE

Try this experiment to see how air contracts and expands depending on how hot or cold it is.

You will need:

- A plastic bottle
- A balloon
- A refrigerator
- A sink with hot water (not too hot to touch)

1

Stretch the neck of the balloon over the top of the bottle, pulling it down well.

2

Fill the sink with hot water. Hold the bottle in the water up to its neck for a few minutes. What happens to the balloon?

3

You should see that as the air in the bottle heats up, it expands and blows up the balloon. Now put the bottle in the refrigerator for ten minutes.

4

What has happened to the balloon? You should see that as the air in the bottle cools, it shrinks and sucks the balloon inside the bottle.

What are forces?

Forces make things move, stop, or change shape, speed, or direction. Whenever you push, pull, twist, or squish something, you are using forces.

Some forces can be seen, such as when you throw a ball, but others, such as magnetic force, are invisible.

Resistance is a dragging force. Air resistance slows down the ball.

You throw the ball to make it move.

PULL

PUSH

PUSH

Would you use a PUSH or a PULL force to do the things below?

1
PUSH ☐
PULL ☐

2
PUSH ☐
PULL ☐

3
PUSH ☐
PULL ☐

4
PUSH ☐
PULL ☐

Pressure is a pressing force. The weight of the player presses on the grass and flattens it.

Gravity

When you drop something—splat!—it falls to the floor. No surprises there, but why do things always fall to the ground? Well, that's all down to a force called gravity.

Gravity is why we don't just float off into space.

A massive object like the Earth has a lot of gravity. It pulls everything nearby toward it.

It feels to us as if gravity pulls things *down*. But gravity really affects all objects and makes them pull toward each other.

PULL

The Earth's gravity attracts everything from a ball to the Moon!

Wherever you are on Earth, its gravity pulls you toward the center of the planet.

EXPERIMENT ZONE

 Experiment with gravity! Does a heavy object fall faster than a light object?

You will need:

- Two sheets of paper
- A tennis ball or similar

1 Crumple up one of the sheets of paper until it is roughly the same size as the ball.

Gravity pulls the ball down more strongly, but you should find that they land at the same time!

2 Which one feels heavier, the ball or the crumpled paper?

Which one do you think will hit the ground first?

3 Time to test your theory! Drop both from the same height and at the same time. What happens?

4 Now try the flat sheet of paper and the crumpled ball of paper. What happens?

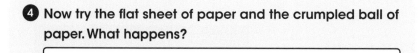

GRAVITY   GRAVITY

AIR RESISTANCE   AIR RESISTANCE

The sheet of paper should land last because its flat shape gets more resistance from the air.

A balancing act

Every object has a center of gravity. This is the point on which an object or person can balance. Objects or people tip over when their center of gravity is not in line with their base.

The girl on tiptoe has a narrow base. She's balanced, but her center of gravity could easily come out of line with her base, tipping her over.

The boy has a wide base and looks very stable.

Can you twirl on the spot and keep your balance like me?

Center of gravity

Wide base

Center of gravity

Narrow base

Whoa!

Center of gravity

This dancer's center of gravity is outside her base, so she is going to fall!

Base

EXPERIMENT ZONE

You will need:
- Two forks
- A large coin
- A glass

Can you balance a coin on the edge of a glass?

The forks act like the balancing pole of a tightrope walker.

They move the center of gravity from the middle of the coin to its edge!

1 Carefully fit the forks onto the edge of the coin. Make sure they are securely attached.

2 Balance the coin on the edge of the glass, moving it around until you find its center of gravity.

Friction

Have you noticed that it's hard work to drag a heavy box across the floor? That's because of friction—a gripping force that happens when two things rub together.

It's easier to slide down a smooth slide than a rough grassy slope.

Smooth, shiny surfaces have less friction, while rough ones have more.

Friction between the rubber tires and the ground help to push a bicycle along.

Friction makes things slow down. Your brakes grip the wheels and use friction to slow you down.

EXPERIMENT ZONE

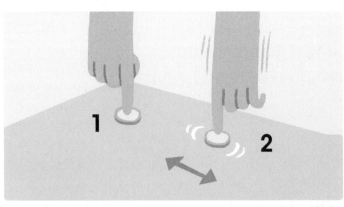

Want to feel how friction heats things up? Try this experiment!

You will need:

- Two identical coins
- A large pad of paper

1 Put the coins on the paper and put your fingertips on them.

2 Hold coin 1 still. Rub coin 2 backward and forward on the paper as fast as you can for 20 seconds. Pick up both coins. Which one feels hotter?

3 You should find that coin 2 feels hotter. That's because friction between the paper and the coin has turned the movement energy into heat.

Friction also creates heat. Your brakes get hot when you use them.

A rubber shoe sole keeps your feet from slipping off your skateboard!

Friction can help keep things from slipping.

Wheels work!

Long ago, people moved heavy things by just dragging them. Friction made this very hard work! Around 5,500 years ago, the wheel was invented, which made moving things around much easier!

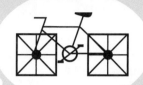

Whoa! The wheel is my favorite invention!

What's the best shape for wheels?

Circles! They're the same shape whichever way up they are, so they roll easily.

INVENTING THE WHEEL

The force of friction makes it difficult to drag things along the ground.

This job is a real drag!

Wheels were developed when people realized that it was easier to move objects that roll.

Hey! That gives me an idea!

Draw as many things that have wheels as you can in the space below. How many can you think of?

So people put objects on top of logs and rolled them along. But this still wasn't that easy.

Later, people fitted wheels that could spin around freely on carts—this really caught on.

Under pressure

You may not notice it, but you are under pressure! The air above you has a weight that presses down. This force is called air pressure.

There is a layer of air all around the Earth called the atmosphere.

PRESS

The higher you go, the less air there is above you.

PRESS

The air pressure at the top of a hill or mountain is lower than it is at sea level.

PRESS

All the time, air is pressing down on us. We don't usually notice it, because we're used to it.

There is more air pressing down on you at sea level.

Water is heavier than air and presses down harder. The deeper you go, the greater the water pressure. Deep-sea animals are used to it, but humans need strong submarines to protect them from being squashed!

A strange-looking fish is following me!

EXPERIMENT ZONE

Discover how air, although it is invisible, puts pressure on objects.

You will need:
- A plastic bottle
- A small piece of paper towel

1

Lay the bottle down on a table. Roll the paper towel into a tight ball, and place it inside the opening of the bottle.

2

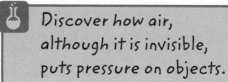

Now see if you can blow the ball into the bottle. What happens?

When you blow, you're putting even more air in the bottle, and this pushes the paper ball back out!

Although the bottle looks empty, it's really full of air.

Float your boat

Why do some things float and others sink? A boat floats because the water beneath it pushes up to balance the weight of the boat pressing down.

Whether an object floats depends on how heavy it is for its size—how dense it is.

Things float if they are lighter than the same volume of water.

Weight of boat

Water pressing up

Things sink when they are denser than water.

An anchor is heavier than the same volume of water. The water cannot hold it up, so it sinks.

Tick which three of these objects you think might float.

Seashell

Cork

Pebble

Coin

Apple

Wooden ice pop stick

EXPERIMENT ZONE

 Try this experiment to make a raisin sink and float.

You will need:
- A bottle of soda water
- A tall, clear glass
- A raisin

① Fill the glass with soda water and drop the raisin in. It should sink to the bottom.

② Watch for a while and see what happens. The raisin should rise. But why?

The raisin is denser than water, so at first it sinks.

Then gas bubbles stick to the raisin. These make it less dense and help it float!

At the surface, the bubbles pop, and the raisin sinks again!

Going up!

Things can float in the air as well as in water. Hot air is less dense than cold air, so the air pressure around a hot-air balloon lifts it up into the sky.

Hot air takes up more space than cold air because as air heats up, it spreads out and gets bigger.

That means a balloon full of hot air is less dense than the colder air around it—which makes it float.

Today, balloons are made out of nylon or polyester that is difficult to tear.

55

Magnetic force

Have you ever wondered how refrigerator magnets stick? It's thanks to an invisible force called magnetism. This force lets a magnet attract some metal objects, including the steel door of a refrigerator.

EXPERIMENT ZONE

Use a magnet to make a paper clip chain, and see how attraction passes from one metal to another.

You will need:

- A toy magnet or refrigerator magnet
- Steel paper clips

1 Place a paper clip close to the magnet. Feel the pull, then let go.

2 Try adding another paper clip at the bottom of the first one. Can you make a chain?

3 The stronger the magnet, the more paper clips you will be able to add!

When it comes to magnets, opposites really attract!

Magnetic force can even work through other objects. A magnet can attract a paper clip through a piece of paper.

Magnetic forces are strongest at the two ends, or poles, of a magnet.

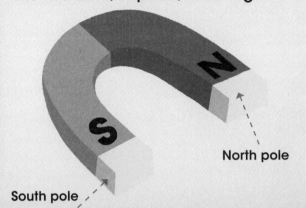

North pole

South pole

The north pole of one magnet will attract the south pole of the other.

Two matching poles will push each other away, or **repel** each other.

Not all metals can be pulled by a magnet, but iron, steel, cobalt, and nickel can.

When a magnet pulls on a metal object, that object becomes magnetic, too.

Magnets can be used to test if objects are made of metals such as steel or iron.

Rocket science!

How does a rocket blast off? A rocket works by pushing out a jet of gas. As the gas shoots out one way, it forces the rocket to move the other way.

A rocket like this has enough pushing power to get it into space.

The fastest rocket to launch was the New Horizons space probe. Soon after takeoff in 2006, it reached a speed of more than 36,350 mph.

Gas gets pushed down ...

... rocket gets pushed up!

When a force pushes one way, there is an equal push back the other way.

Space rockets make the gas by burning lots of fuel.

EXPERIMENT ZONE

Discover the forces behind rocket science by making your own balloon rocket.

The balloon squeezes out the air to power it along!

You will need:

- A balloon
- Tape
- A drinking straw
- A ball of thin string or thread
- A watch or timer

1 Thread the straw onto the string. Tie or tape the string across the room.

2 Blow up the balloon and hold the opening so that the air can't escape. While you hold the balloon, tape it onto the straw as shown.

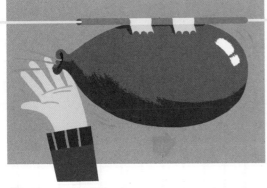

3 Move the balloon along to the end of the string. Then, 5, 4, 3, 2, 1 ... let go!

Balloon rocket results

1 Time how fast your rocket moved across the room.

[   ] seconds

2 Can you make a second balloon rocket and race them? Who won?

[   ]

3 Try setting up the string so that it's pointing straight up. How high does the rocket go?

[   ]

Material world

Look around you. What do you see? There's stuff everywhere! Houses, trees, bicycles, food—even your own body—it's all made of stuff that scientists call "matter."

Strong, waterproof plastic

Different types of matter are known as materials. They can be hard or soft, shiny or dull, solid or liquid, bendy or strong.

The ways materials look and behave are called their properties—the things that make them useful for different jobs.

Glass is strong and see-through, which makes it useful for windows that let in light.

Strong ston

Look around your house and see how many useful materials you can see.

Some things, such as a wooden table, are made of one material.

Other things are made of many materials. For example, a television is made of glass, metal, and plastic.

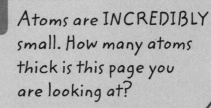

Atoms are INCREDIBLY small. How many atoms thick is this page you are looking at?

1. 1,000,000 atoms
2. 1,000 atoms
3. 1 atom

Warm, flexible fabric

Atoms

If you could look REALLY close up, you'd see that all materials are made of tiny particles, called atoms.

There are many different types of atoms. Some are bigger than others, but all are much too small to see!

Hard wood

Atoms join together in different ways to form differrent kinds of molecules. Molecules are the building blocks of matter.

Sorting stuff

Artificial materials are made by changing things found in nature, for example by heating them.

One of the jobs scientists do is to sort (classify) things. One way to sort materials is by how they are made. Some are found in nature, such as wood. Others, such as plastic, are made by people.

Check off the natural materials.

Paper is made from mashed-up wood treated with chemicals.

 Paper

Plastic

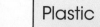 Diamond

Glass is made by heating rock and sand.

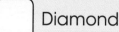

 Wool

Tree bark

 Rubber

 Glass

☐ Leather

Plastic ☐

☐ Flower

Bricks are made from clay.

Cat fur ☐

☐ Wood

☐ Brick

Cotton is made from plant fibers.

☐ Cotton

Objects that are made from natural materials are still natural. A wooden table is still a natural material.

☐ Gold

Seashell ☐

Testing, testing!

Time to get hands-on with materials! Find out what properties everyday materials have by testing them. Experiment and discover more about how different materials behave.

EXPERIMENT ZONE

Gather some materials, then try the tests below to find out some of their properties.

Check with a grown-up before you test anything. You could even get them to be your assistant!

You will need:

- A dishpan full of water
- A metal spoon
- A wooden spoon
- A sheet of white paper
- A sponge
- A metal paper clip
- A rubber band
- A magnet

1 Does it float or sink?

2 Is it flexible or rigid? Will it stretch or bend?

3 Is it rough or smooth?

4 Is it pulled by a magnet?
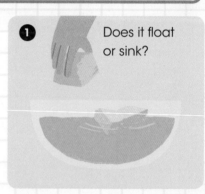

5

How strong is it? Could you break or tear it?

6

Is it hard or soft?

7 Is it see-through? Can you shine a light through it?

Cool! Transparent materials let light through.

64

TEST RESULTS

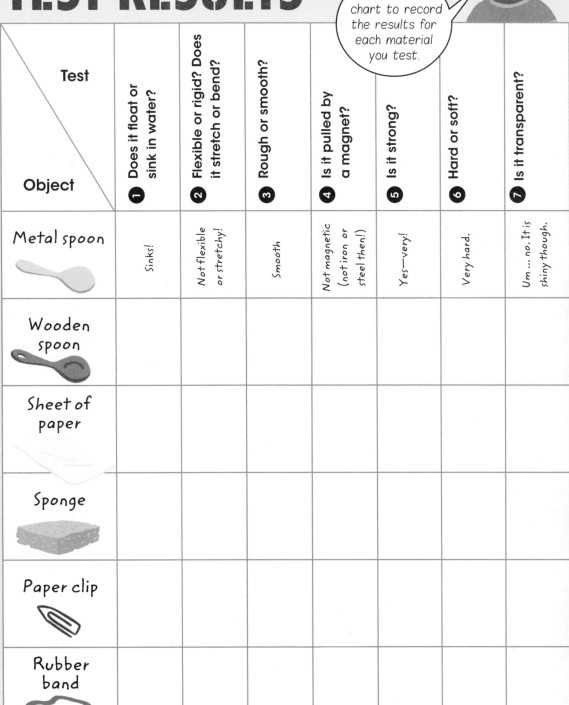

Use the chart to record the results for each material you test.

Test \ Object	**1** Does it float or sink in water?	**2** Flexible or rigid? Does it stretch or bend?	**3** Rough or smooth?	**4** Is it pulled by a magnet?	**5** Is it strong?	**6** Hard or soft?	**7** Is it transparent?
Metal spoon	Sinks!	Not flexible or stretchy!	Smooth	Not magnetic (not iron or steel then!)	Yes—very!	Very hard.	Um...no. It is shiny though.
Wooden spoon							
Sheet of paper							
Sponge							
Paper clip							
Rubber band							

Kitchen chemistry

Did you know that your kitchen is a secret laboratory? When you bake a cake, different materials get mixed up and heated to make something new. That's a chemical reaction!

In a chemical reaction, the atoms from each material rearrange themselves into new materials, made from the same ingredients.

Baking a cake uses chemical reactions.

Water and sugar are everyday chemicals.

Chemicals are materials that are the same all the way through.

Baking powder contains two chemicals that react together to make bubbles of gas in the cake batter.

As the cake bakes, the gas bubbles expand. This makes the cake rise and gives it a spongy texture.

EXPERIMENT ZONE

 Ask an adult to help with this experiment. Wear kitchen gloves, and do everything in the kitchen sink.

You will need:
- Kitchen gloves
- A see-through glass
- Food coloring
- Baking powder
- White vinegar
- Dishwashing liquid

 This chemistry experiment lets you see gas being made by a chemical reaction.

1 Stand the glass in the sink and add several spoonfuls of baking powder.

2 Squirt a small amount of dishwashing liquid on top. Next, add a few drops of food coloring.

3 Pour in some vinegar until the glass is about a quarter full.

4 Watch what happens. You should see your experiment mixture bubble over with colorful froth!

 Wow! A chemical reaction between the baking powder and vinegar creates carbon dioxide gas.

 The gas gets trapped inside the dishwashing liquid bubbles.

Fireworks!

Whoosh! Bang! Fireworks are amazing, but just how do they work? Well, it's all down to chemistry. Burning is a type of chemical reaction, and you can see it in action at a firework display!

Burning is a chemical reaction that happens between a fuel, such as wood, and oxygen in the air.

Burning changes the wood into smoke and flames. The fuel won't stop burning until it's all used up.

Scientists call burning combustion.

When a firework is lit, the chemicals inside burn very fast, making an explosion.

The gases produced by burning shoot a firework into the air, just like a space rocket.

The chemicals in fireworks burn with bright white or colored light.

Color the shapes to create your own colorful firework display. Add some more starry bursts!

The acid test

Ever tasted a lemon? Lemons taste sour because lemon juice is an acid. The chemical opposite of an acid is an alkali. Most everyday substances are one or the other.

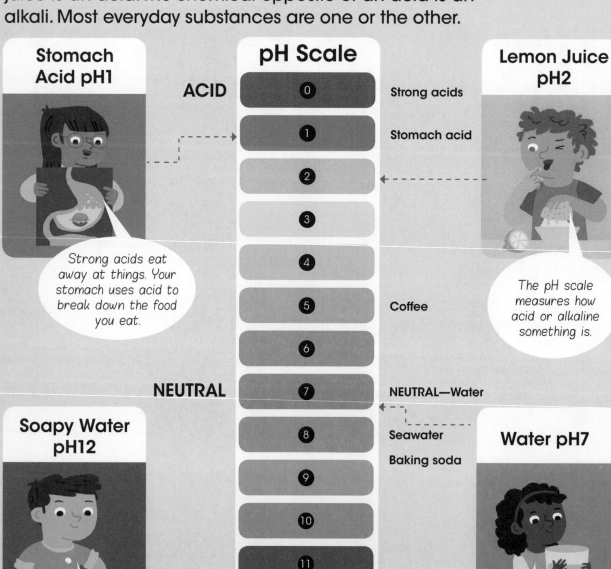

Stomach Acid pH1

Strong acids eat away at things. Your stomach uses acid to break down the food you eat.

pH Scale

ACID

0	Strong acids
1	Stomach acid
2	
3	
4	
5	Coffee
6	

NEUTRAL

7	NEUTRAL—Water
8	Seawater
9	Baking soda
10	
11	
12	Soapy water
13	Bleach
14	Strong alkalis

ALKALI

Lemon Juice pH2

The pH scale measures how acid or alkaline something is.

Soapy Water pH12

I didn't know that dishwashing water was an alkali!

Water pH7

Water is neutral. Acids and alkalis can cancel each other out to become neutral.

EXPERIMENT ZONE

Using a red cabbage, you can test which substances are acid and which are alkali.

Scientists use chemicals called indicators to test if things are acid or alkali.

You will need:

- Red cabbage
- Hot tap water
- A pitcher
- A strainer
- A wooden spoon
- Four clear plastic cups
- Substances to test: baking powder, soapy water, lemon juice, and water

1 Tear some red cabbage leaves into pieces and put them into a pitcher. Carefully add hot tap water and stir with a wooden spoon.

2 When the water turns deep red, use the strainer to strain a small amount into four cups.

Baking powder   Soapy water   Lemon juice   Water

3 Add a small amount of each substance to the cabbage water, and note the results.

If your indicator turns more red, it shows an acid, more blue an alkali, and no change means neutral. Write your results here!

	Acid	Alkali	Neutral
Baking powder			
Soapy water			
Lemon juice			
Water			

Solid, liquid, gas

Matter isn't just hard, solid stuff. It's also liquids or gases. In fact, solid, liquid, and gas are the three main forms or 'states' that matter can take.

Most gases are invisible—but you can see them when they form bubbles in sodas.

You can see all three states of matter here. The plate and the glass are solid. The soda is a liquid, but the bubbles in it are a gas.

What makes a material a solid, liquid, or gas? It's all to do with how it behaves and what the tiny particles it is made from are doing.

SOLID PLATE

GAS BUBBLES

LIQUID DRINK

Doodle lots of colored bubbles here!

You can see solid, liquid, and gas in action when you blow bubbles.

The bubble jar, lid, and wand are solid and keep their shape.

The bubble mixture is liquid. It fills up the jar and drips off the wand!

When you blow a bubble, you fill it with your breath (made of gas).

LIQUIDS
Liquids can pour, splash, and flow. Their particles can move freely around to fill the shape of containers, such as a glass.

SOLIDS
Solids keep their shape. Their particles are packed closely together and stay fixed in place.

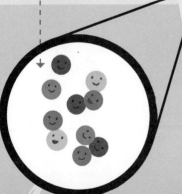

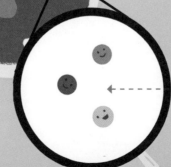

GASES
Gases spread out to fill the space they are in. Their particles move about very fast and are far apart.

Changing state

Do you know where rain comes from? OK, it DOES come from the sky, but it's also due to water changing state from liquid to gas—and back again! This is called the water cycle.

1 Rain falls from heavy clouds, forming puddles, and filling rivers, lakes, ponds, and the sea.

3 The water vapor rises up into the air, where it cools down and turns back into liquid water droplets. These form clouds.

2 When the sun comes out, it heats up the water. When it gets hot enough, the water changes from liquid into water vapor, a gas.

GAS

LIQUID

When water changes from liquid to gas, we say it evaporates.

EXPERIMENT ZONE

Try this experiment to see the changing states of water.

You will need:

- A large spoon
- Salt
- Water
- A pan
- Black paper
- A cookie sheet
- A magnifying glass

1 Add several large spoons of salt to some water in a pan and stir until all the salt has dissolved.

2 Lay the black paper on a cookie sheet, and pour in enough salt water to cover the paper.

The heat changes the water from liquid into vapor, leaving the solid salt crystals behind.

3 Put the cookie sheet somewhere warm, such as outside in the sun or on a table by a window. Wait for the water to evaporate. Then look closely with a magnifying glass!

Incredible ice

Water is weird! Most liquids get smaller when they freeze—their particles move closer together as they change into a solid. But when water freezes into solid ice, it expands, taking up more space.

Because ice takes up more space than water, it is less dense (lighter for its size) than water, and so it floats.

So that's why icebergs and ice cubes float!

When water freezes, the particles form a network and push apart. This means they take up more space.

ICE

Water freezes into ice at a temperature of 32 degrees Fahrenheit (32°F).

EXPERIMENT ZONE

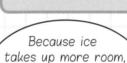 Try this experiment to prove that water expands when it freezes.

You will need:

- Two small plastic cups (the same size)
- Water
- A freezer

Because ice takes up more room, the water in cup 2 will fill more of the cup as solid ice.

1 Cup 1 · Cup 2

Fill the cups half full—make sure the water level is exactly the same in both.

2 32°F · Cup 1 · Cup 2

Put cup 2 in the freezer, and leave cup 1 in the kitchen. Leave the cups overnight.

3 Cup 1 · Cup 2

Next day, take cup 2 out of the freezer and compare it with cup 1. What has happened?

Skating on water

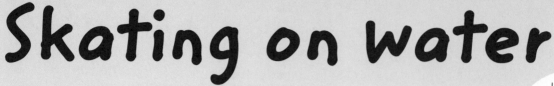

You may have been ice skating, but pond skating is definitely not a good idea! Yet small insects CAN skate across liquid water. How do they do that?

Wow! The surface of the water doesn't break.

This pond skater's feet are pressing down on the water. But why don't they poke through?

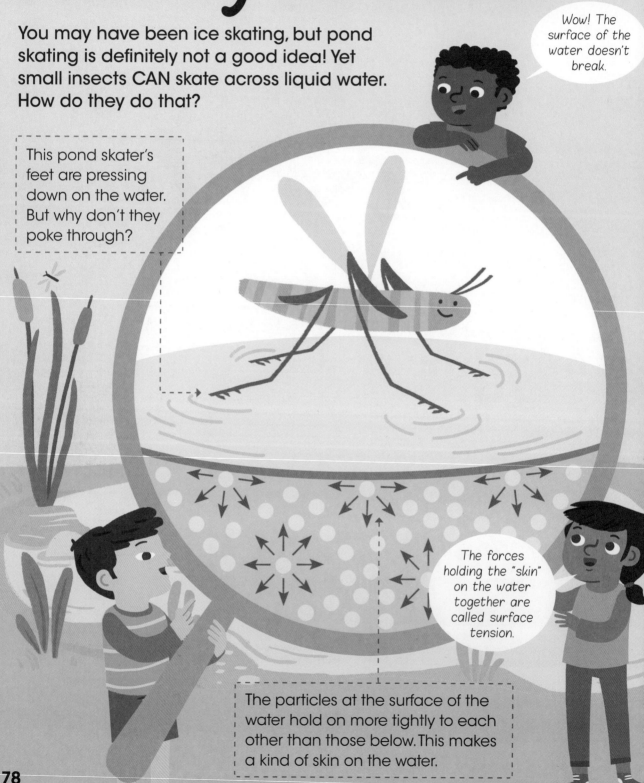

The forces holding the "skin" on the water together are called surface tension.

The particles at the surface of the water hold on more tightly to each other than those below. This makes a kind of skin on the water.

EXPERIMENT ZONE

 Try these two experiments to examine surface tension for yourself.

You will need:

- A small coin
- A bowl
- A paper clip
- Water
- Paper towel

1 Use your fingertip to drop water drops onto the coin, one at a time. The water doesn't run off right away because of surface tension. How high can you make your bulging drop of water?

2 Use surface tension to carefully lay a paper clip on the surface of a bowl of water. It's easier if you put a small piece of paper towel under it first.

Raindrops on a window don't spread out flat. They stay round. That's also because of surface tension!

Smart science

The next time you take a bath, watch how the water level rises when you get in. Noticing this helped an ancient Greek scientist named Archimedes solve a tricky problem.

According to legend, Archimedes needed to measure the volume of a golden crown—how much space it took up. But he didn't know how.

While puzzling over this problem, Archimedes got in the bathtub. He saw the water level rise.

Suddenly, he realized that if you put something in water, water flows around it, pushing up the water level.

When Archimedes found the answer, he shouted "EUREKA," which means "I've found it!"

One milliliter of water has a volume of one cubic centimeter. There are 200 cubic centimeters of water in this beaker.

300 ml

200 ml

100 ml

Archimedes saw that if you measure the volume of water in a jar, then add an object to it and measure again, the difference will be equal to the object's volume.

Let's add some pebbles to the water!

The water level has risen by 100 milliliters.

300 ml

200 ml

100 ml

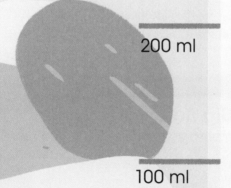

That means the volume of space taken up by the pebbles is 100 cubic centimeters.

Figure out the volume of a crown using Archimedes' method.

A beaker of water is filled up with 500 ml of water. When the crown is dropped into the water, the volume increases to 600 ml.

How much has the water level increased?

_____ ml

What is the volume of the crown?

_____ cm³

Discovering Earth

Our world is amazing! Scientists have discovered lots about Earth, including what it is made of and how it was formed. But Earth is just one planet in a huge universe, and scientists study that, too!

Planet Earth is totally amazing!

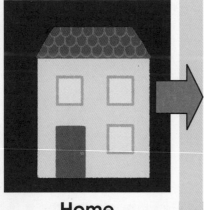

Home

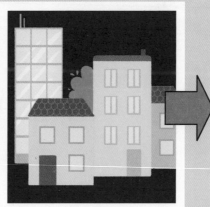

Town

Country

So where does the **Earth** fit into the universe? Just imagine zooming out from where you live to see the BIGGER picture!

When the universe started, it was smaller than the head of a pin, but it soon grew much bigger!

The Big Bang

Scientists think the universe formed in a huge explosion known as the Big Bang that happened about 14 billion years ago.

The Milky Way is just one of billions of galaxies scattered through the universe.

Universe

Earth, along with other planets, orbits (travels around) a star called the Sun.

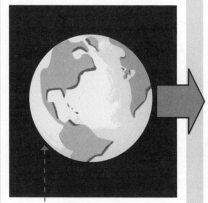

Planet

Solar system

Galaxy

Earth is a small rocky planet in the **solar system**.

The **Sun** is just one of billions of stars in our galaxy, the **Milky Way**.

Draw a picture of where you live. Then add your FULL address!

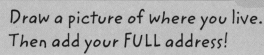

House: ....

Town/City: ....

Country: ....

Planet: ....

The Solar System,

The Milky Way, the Universe.

Looking at space

When you look at the night sky, you are looking into space! There are many amazing things in space, including planets, stars, and galaxies. Scientists who study them are called astronomers.

Stars are huge balls of hot gas. They are so far away that they look like dots of light.

MOONS

Moons are balls of rock that orbit planets.

Our **Sun** looks bigger than the other stars because it is a LOT closer than they are.

STARS

The Sun is the closest star to Earth. It's just 93 million miles away!

GALAXIES

The name "planet" means "wanderer."

Planets are worlds a little like Earth. They orbit the Sun.

PLANETS

Galaxies are huge spinning clusters of stars.

Connect the dots, then identify the constellation.

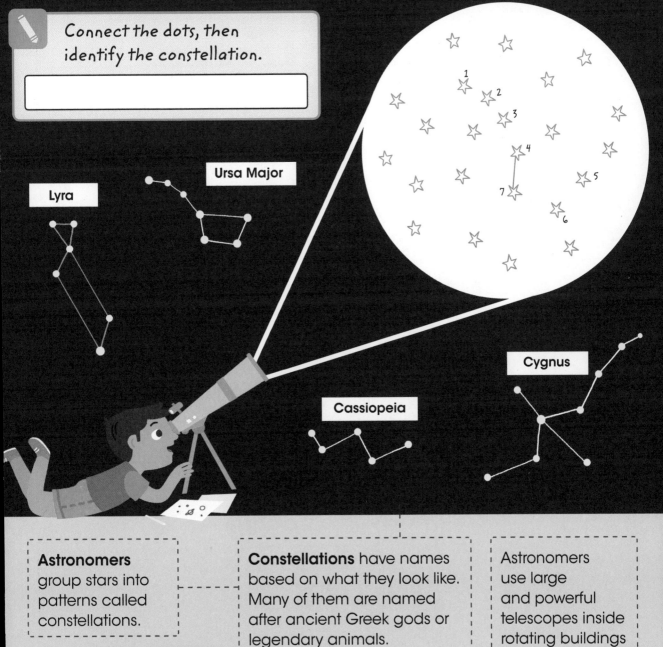

Lyra

Ursa Major

Cygnus

Cassiopeia

Astronomers group stars into patterns called constellations.

Constellations have names based on what they look like. Many of them are named after ancient Greek gods or legendary animals.

Astronomers use large and powerful telescopes inside rotating buildings to see farther into space. They also use telescopes in space.

Solar System

Our solar system is our own local neighborhood in space. It is made up of the Sun and eight different planets, their moons, and asteroids and comets.

Mars looks red because of the rusty red rocks and volcanoes on its surface.

Mars

Mercury

Venus

Mercury is a small, rocky planet and is the closest to the Sun.

Venus is the hottest planet and is covered by clouds of thick gases.

Earth

Our Moon orbits the Earth just as Earth orbits the Sun.

Our world, Earth, looks blue from space because it is covered by water.

The Sun is a ball of hot gas that gives off heat and light.

Chunks of rock called asteroids also orbit the Sun.

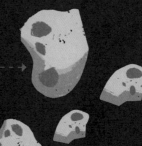

Saturn

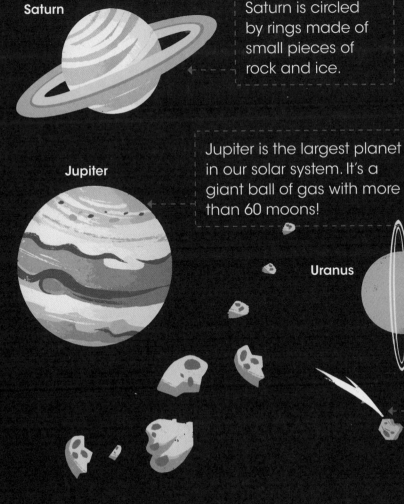

Saturn is circled by rings made of small pieces of rock and ice.

Neptune is a very cold, blue planet with more than 13 moons.

Neptune

Jupiter

Jupiter is the largest planet in our solar system. It's a giant ball of gas with more than 60 moons!

Uranus

Uranus is a cold, icy gas world with giant rings around it.

Comets are balls of rock and ice. They glow when they come close to the Sun.

EXPERIMENT ZONE

The Sun and the planets are huge distances apart. Try this to see how big our solar system is.

You will need:

● A honeydew melon

● A peppercorn

1 Ask a friend to stand still holding the melon. Take 25 big steps away from your friend.

2 Turn around and hold up the peppercorn. The peppercorn represents Earth, and the melon is the Sun!

25 steps

Magnetic Earth

Earth has a rocky crust and a solid iron core. Between them is the mantle, containing melted rock, or magma. The iron core creates a magnetic field around Earth that reaches out into space.

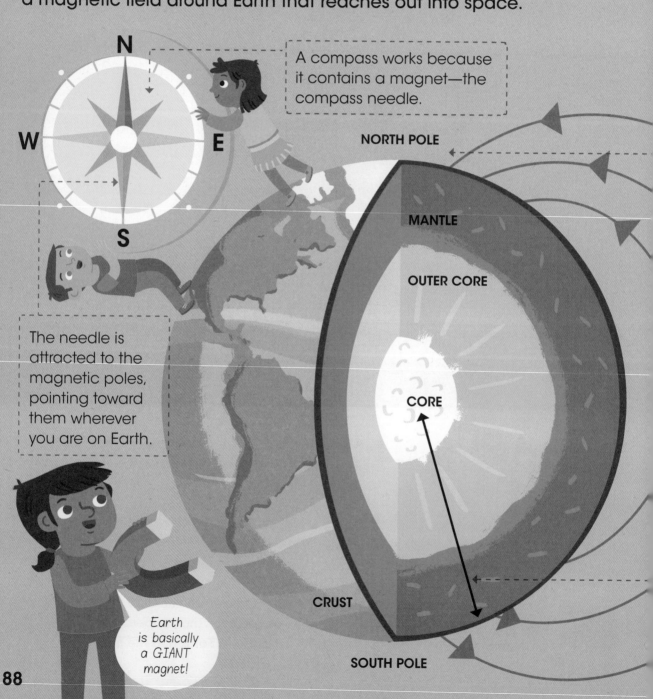

A compass works because it contains a magnet—the compass needle.

NORTH POLE

MANTLE

OUTER CORE

CORE

The needle is attracted to the magnetic poles, pointing toward them wherever you are on Earth.

CRUST

Earth is basically a GIANT magnet!

SOUTH POLE

Earth's magnetic field curves around near the poles and stretches far out into space.

The north end of a magnet (N) is attracted to the Earth's North Pole.

MAGNETIC FIELD

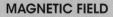

The measurement from the Earth's crust to its center is 3,959 miles.

EXPERIMENT ZONE

You will need:

- A needle
- A bar magnet
- A circle of cork
- Poster tack
- A shallow dish of water

Make a simple compass to see the effect of Earth's magnetic field.

① Stroke the needle from the end to the tip with the north end of a bar magnet about 50 times. This will magnetize the needle.

TIP

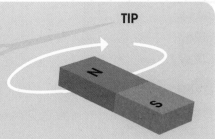

② Ask a grown-up to help you stick the magnetized needle across a circle of cork with sticky tack.

③ Float the cork in a dish of water. What happens? Rotate the dish. Does the direction of the needle change?

The tip of the needle will always try to point to the North Pole of the Earth.

NORTH

The needle has been turned into a magnet.

Rocks and minerals

Earth's crust contains thousands of different types of minerals. Rocks are usually made up of different types of minerals mixed together. Both can be very useful!

Scientists sort minerals by how hard they are and how well they reflect light.

Flint was used long ago to make sharp tools.

Quartz and chalk are common minerals.

Sandstone, slate, and granite are rocks used for building.

Chalk is very soft and nonreflective, while diamond is very hard and reflective.

Copper and gold are both metals, a type of mineral.

Limestone is often found in caves.

Diamonds, emeralds, and rubies are rare minerals.

Water wears rocks smooth to form pebbles.

Rocks and minerals are not alive!

Only around 30 minerals are common. The others are rarely found.

Earth scientists who study rocks and minerals are called **geologists**.

? Which of the following is a metal found in the Earth? Check the correct answer below:

❶ Slate ☐
❷ Limestone ☐
❸ Gold ☐

Salt crystals

Crystals aren't just found in rocks; they are all around us every day. For example, snowflakes, diamonds, and salt are all types of crystal. So what are crystals, and how do they form?

In a crystal, the tiny particles fit together in regular patterns, forming geometric shapes.

Salt crystals are the shape of cubes.

Crystals like salt can form blocks with very smooth, flat faces called facets.

Crystals have sharp edges, too.

SALT CRYSTAL

EXPERIMENT ZONE

 Make salt crystals with this fun experiment!

You will need:
- A glass jar
- Hot tap water
- Table salt
- A tablespoon
- An ice pop stick
- String

1 Fill the jar three-quarters full with hot water.

2 Stir in salt, and keep adding more until it no longer disappears.

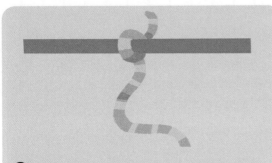

3 Tie a short piece of string to the ice pop stick.

4 Lay the stick on top of the jar, so that the string dangles into the liquid.

5 Leave in a safe, still, cool place for a few days. Watch what happens.

Crystals should form on the string!

Look at them with a magnifying glass. What shape are they?

Quicksand

If sand is mixed with clay and water, it becomes quicksand. Quicksand is a material that can behave like both a solid and a liquid. You can make something similar at home.

EXPERIMENT ZONE

You will need:
- Cornstarch
- A plastic cup
- Water
- A wooden spoon
- A large mixing bowl

Cornstarch Gloop behaves just like quicksand. Make some and discover how it can act like a solid or a liquid!

You may need to add a little more water or cornstarch to get the mix right.

1 Put three cups of cornstarch into the bowl.

2 Add about two cups of water.

3 Mix them together—this takes a while!

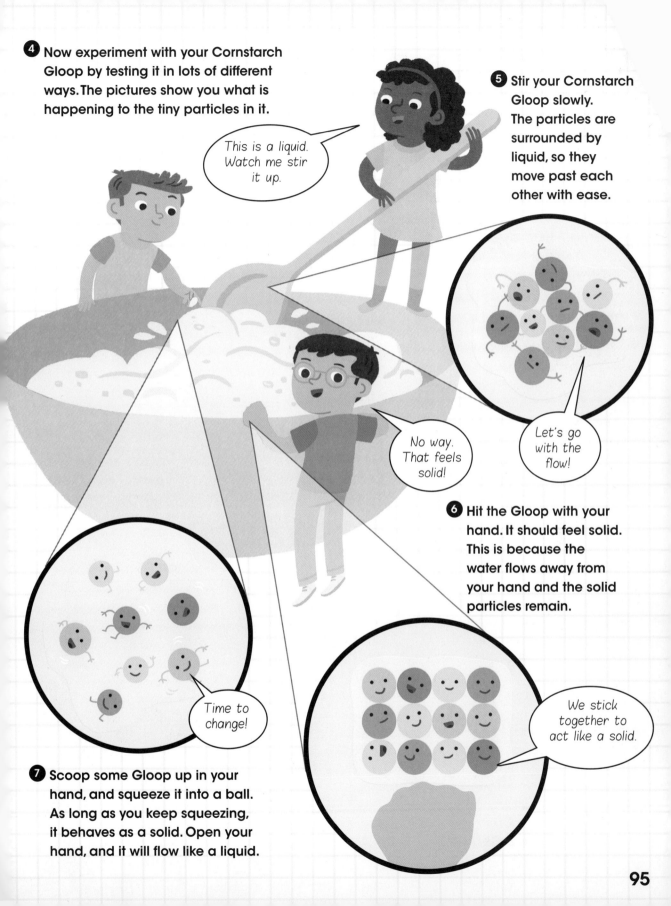

4 Now experiment with your Cornstarch Gloop by testing it in lots of different ways. The pictures show you what is happening to the tiny particles in it.

This is a liquid. Watch me stir it up.

5 Stir your Cornstarch Gloop slowly. The particles are surrounded by liquid, so they move past each other with ease.

No way. That feels solid!

Let's go with the flow!

6 Hit the Gloop with your hand. It should feel solid. This is because the water flows away from your hand and the solid particles remain.

Time to change!

We stick together to act like a solid.

7 Scoop some Gloop up in your hand, and squeeze it into a ball. As long as you keep squeezing, it behaves as a solid. Open your hand, and it will flow like a liquid.

olcano science

Watch out—this volcano is about to erupt! Scientists study volcanoes to discover how they work, as well as when and where a volcanic eruption might happen.

Scientists who study volcanoes are called **volcanologists**. They visit active volcanoes to collect gas or lava, and to measure volcanic activity.

This suit helps to protect me from the heat!

Volcanoes form where hot, molten rock called magma bursts through the Earth's crust. If you could cut a volcano in half, this is what you would see.

The molten rock that comes pouring out is called lava.

As well as lava, volcanoes pour out hot gas, ash, dust, and big lumps of rock.

At first, the lava is so hot, it is a flowing liquid, but when it cools, it turns into solid rock.

VENT

FINISH

Magma flows
from the magma
chamber through
tunnels called
pipes, to vents on
the surface.

PIPE

Magma is very hot
liquid rock, around
1832°F—much,
much hotter than
a hot oven!

MAGMA
CHAMBER

START

Use a red pen and color in
a path from the magma
chamber to a vent.

Weather watch

One big question for scientists is ... will it rain tomorrow?!
To figure out what the weather might be, they measure it with
all kinds of equipment. Make your own weather station!

EXPERIMENT ZONE

 Make a windstick to find out which way the wind is blowing.

1. Attach colorful strips of paper to the top of your stick using tape.

2. Push the stick into the ground.

3. On a windy day, watch the direction the strips are flying. Use a compass to see where the wind is coming from.

WIND DIRECTION

You will need:

- A straight stick 20 inches long
- Tape
- Strips of colored paper
- A compass

> So, the wind is blowing from the west!

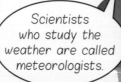
> Scientists who study the weather are called meteorologists.

RAINFALL

 Measure how much rain has fallen with this rain gauge.

You will need:

- A large plastic bottle
- Packaging tape
- Stones
- Marker pen
- Water
- Ruler

1. Cut the top off the bottle about a third of the way down (ask an adult to help). Put a few stones in the bottom. Turn the top upside down, fit it inside the bottle, and tape together.

 2. Use a marker and a ruler to draw a scale on the bottle, in centimeters. Start just above the stones. Then add water until it reaches "0."

AIR PRESSURE

 Make a simple barometer to measure air pressure.

You will need:
- A jar
- A balloon
- A rubber band
- Tape
- A straw

①

Cut the top half off a balloon, and stretch it over the top of the jar (ask an adult to help). Fix it in place with an elastic band.

②

Flatten one end of the straw, and tape it to the middle of the balloon. Stand your barometer outside, somewhere that is sheltered.

③ LOW PRESSURE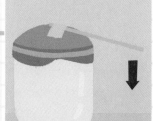

When air pressure is low, the balloon will bulge upward, and your straw will point down.

④ HIGH PRESSURE ⬆

When air pressure is high, it will push down on the balloon, and the straw will point upward.

High pressure usually means calm weather, while low pressure can lead to storms.

Measure how much rain falls in a day— or a week!

③ Stand your rain gauge outside, away from any buildings, where rain can drip into it. After it has rained, count the centimeters of rainfall.

All at sea

Dive in for some sea science! Almost three-quarters of the Earth is covered in water, and most of this is seawater. Take a closer look to really see the sea.

Water is see-through!

As water runs off of hills and mountains and along rivers to the sea, it dissolves minerals from the rocks and soil.

Seawater is a solution. That means that many other small particles are mixed in and flow about freely with the water particles.

One of them is salt, which is why the sea is salty.

Oceanography is the study of sea science.

EXPERIMENT ZONE

You will need:
- Two fresh eggs
- Two large glasses, $3/4$ filled with tap water
- Lots of salt
- A tablespoon

Try this experiment to find out if things float better in salt water than in fresh (nonsalty) water.

❶ Put an egg into each glass of water. What happens? You should see the eggs sink—if they're fresh!

Seawater contains ...

...dissolved gases, such as nitrogen and oxygen, from the air ...

... millions of very tiny creatures, such as plankton and bacteria ...

...and tiny amounts of natural elements, such as gold.

Earth's seas contain about 20 million tons of gold! Unfortunately, it's very difficult to collect.

SALT WATER

FRESH WATER

Hmmm. This experiment is making me hungry!

2 Take an egg out of one glass of water and stir in five tablespoons of salt until it has mostly dissolved.

3 Now try floating the egg again. What happens? You should see the egg float higher in the salty water.

Living science

Earth is home to thousands of different plants and animals. Scientists who study these living things are called biologists. Their first job is to figure out which things are actually alive!

Living things come in all shapes and sizes, but they have lots common!

QUIZ: ARE YOU ALIVE?

You need a YES to ALL of these questions to be alive. Just one NO means it's not a living thing!

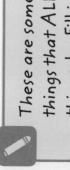

These are some of the things that ALL living things do. Fill in the missing answers on this living things quiz!

ROBOT

PLANT

ANIMAL

1

Does it grow?

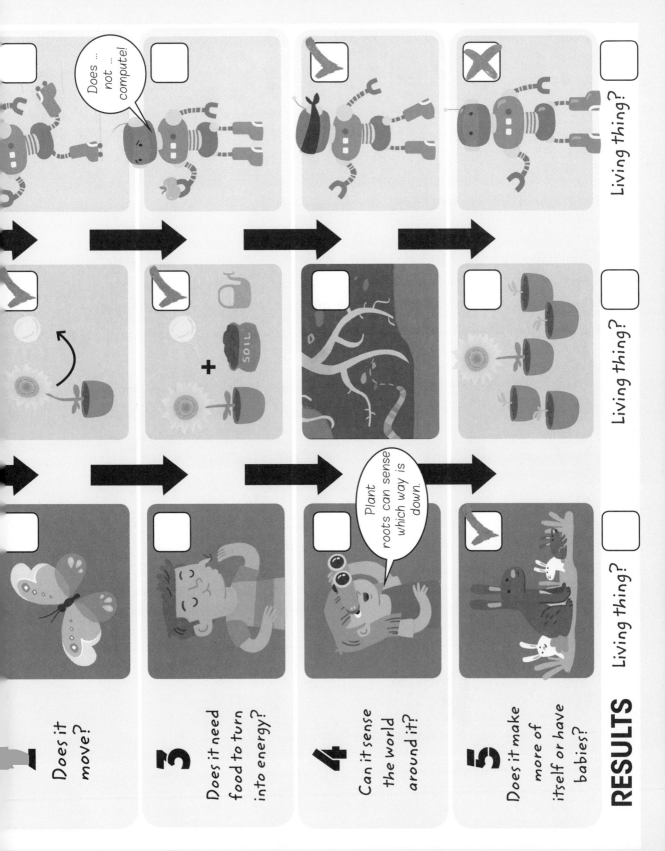

RESULTS   Living thing?   Living thing?   Living thing?

103

Life spotting

Now that you know some of the things that living things do, test your knowledge. Look at the world around you, and see what living and nonliving things you can spot.

Check off the living things.

105

Getting organized

Sorting one living thing from another is called classification. It helps scientists show how different living things are related. Follow the system below to classify a wildcat!

The system we use today was mainly invented by a Swedish scientist, Carl Linnaeus, in the 1730s.

Now we are really getting things sorted out!

ANIMAL KINGDOM

All animals are in the same large group known as the animal kingdom.

VERTEBRATES

INVERTEBRATES

This gets split into ever-smaller groups, such as animals that have backbones (vertebrates) and animals that don't (invertebrates).

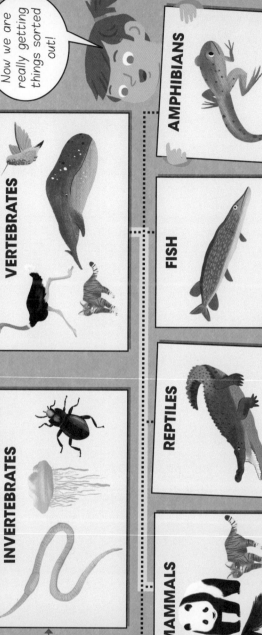

AMPHIBIANS

FISH

REPTILES

MAMMALS

BIRDS

OMNIVORE
(Eats anything!)

There are about one and a half million different types of animal in the animal kingdom.

HERBIVORE
(Plant-eater)

CARNIVORE
(Meat-eater)

FOXES

CATS

BEARS

WILDCAT
(Felis silvestris)

You can sort animals by what they eat, too.

You just keep on dividing, until ...

...you finally get right down to an individual species.

Linnaeus also developed a way of giving each species its own scientific name, written in Latin.

The species name for a wildcat is Felis silvestris, but what does it mean?

1 Very angry cat
2 Cat of the woods
3 Silver cat

Life cycles

Have you ever seen a baby butterfly? No? That's because it looks like a totally different animal—a caterpillar! Some animals, including butterflies, go through amazing changes as they grow.

Hey—you don't look like a butterfly!

1. EGG

A life cycle is a set of life stages a species goes through. A butterfly goes through four stages in its life cycle.

A butterfly lays an egg on a leaf, which will be food for its baby when it hatches.

2. CATERPILLAR

A hungry caterpillar hatches. It has a wriggly body and lots of legs. It eats lots and grows very quickly.

A life cycle can take anything from a few weeks to a few years!

3. CHRYSALIS

When it's fully grown, the caterpillar attaches itself to a twig and forms a hard outer shell called a chrysalis.

Color in this butterfly!

A female adult butterfly will then go on to lay more eggs, and the cycle begins again!

4. ADULT BUTTERFLY

Wow! That's quite a big change.

The chrysalis splits and a fully-grown adult butterfly comes out, ready to fly away!

Body science

Scientists and doctors study the human body to figure out how all its parts work together to help you to live. From head to toe, you are an incredible scientific discovery! Take a tour of your human body now.

Your brain is your body's control center—it helps the rest of the body to work and to do fun stuff like read and understand this book!

Eyes are our windows on the world. They help us to see what's going on.

Muscles help us to move. From working your arms and legs to blinking, it's all muscle power!

Arm muscle

BRAIN

Ears funnel sound to our eardrums, so that we can hear what is going on.

Your body is packed with organs that do special jobs, such as your heart and your lungs.

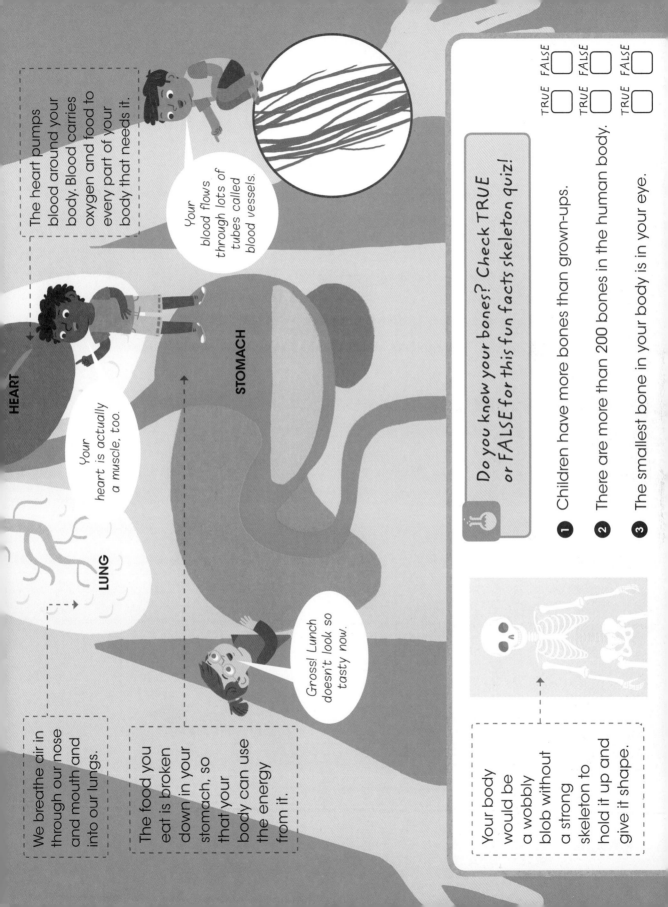

The heart pumps blood around your body. Blood carries oxygen and food to every part of your body that needs it.

HEART

Your heart is actually a muscle, too.

LUNG

We breathe air in through our nose and mouth and into our lungs.

Your blood flows through lots of tubes called blood vessels.

STOMACH

The food you eat is broken down in your stomach, so that your body can use the energy from it.

Gross! Lunch doesn't look so tasty now.

Your body would be a wobbly blob without a strong skeleton to hold it up and give it shape.

Do you know your bones? Check TRUE or FALSE for this fun facts skeleton quiz!

1 Children have more bones than grown-ups.   TRUE ☐ FALSE ☐

2 There are more than 200 bones in the human body.   TRUE ☐ FALSE ☐

3 The smallest bone in your body is in your eye.   TRUE ☐ FALSE ☐

The plant kingdom

Plants belong to one of the other large groups of living things. There are more than 300,000 different types of plant in the plant kingdom! Trees, flowers, vegetables, fruit—we need plants to live!

Plants use the energy from sunlight to turn water and gases from the air into their food.

Leaves make the food chemicals that a plant needs.

SUNLIGHT

Plants can be divided into two groups: those that make flowers and those that don't.

FLOWER

CARBON DIOXIDE GAS

LEAF

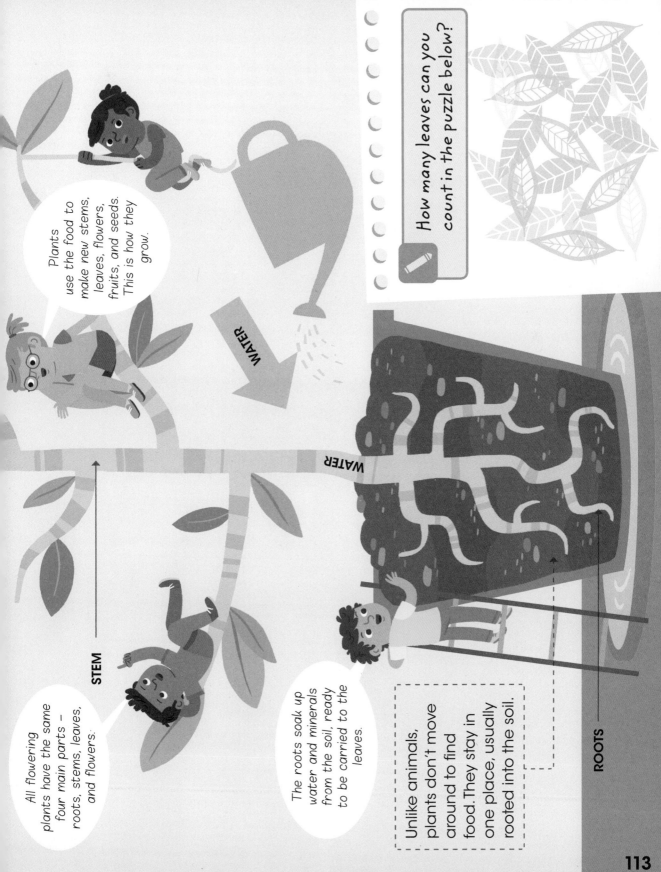

Plants use the food to make new stems, leaves, flowers, fruits, and seeds. This is how they grow.

WATER

WATER

STEM

All flowering plants have the same four main parts – roots, stems, leaves, and flowers.

The roots soak up water and minerals from the soil, ready to be carried to the leaves.

Unlike animals, plants don't move around to find food. They stay in one place, usually rooted into the soil.

ROOTS

How many leaves can you count in the puzzle below?

113

Growing plants

So, just how does your garden grow? For many plants, life begins as a tiny seed. If the seed lands in a good spot, with plenty of soil, water, and light, it starts to grow!

The leaves catch the sunlight, and the seedling starts making food for itself.

Seedlings have just two leaves when they first pop out of the soil.

Shoot

Root

The seed soaks up water and grows. The first root bursts out and starts growing.

Tiny hairs grow from the root—these are what actually take in water from the soil.

Using food stored in the seed, the plant grows toward the surface.

EXPERIMENT ZONE

 Do plants know which way to grow? Try this experiment to find out.

You will need:

- A bean seed (from a package of seeds)
- A clear glass jar
- Paper towel
- Water

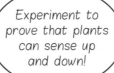 Experiment to prove that plants can sense up and down!

1 Scrunch up some paper towel and line the jar. Push a bean between the paper and the side of the jar.

2 Put the jar on a sunny windowsill. Water it and wait.

 You should see the roots change direction to grow down again!

3 Sprinkle the paper towel with water every day to keep it damp. Wait until the first shoot and root start to grow. Does the root grow down?

4 Turn the jar on its side and leave it. Which way do the roots grow now? Keep turning every week or so to prove your point!

What plants need

Plants need water, right? You'll know that if you've ever forgotten to water one! But how did scientists figure out what plants need to live?

EXPERIMENT ZONE

Let's do some plant science!

 Do plants need BOTH sunlight and water to grow? Find out here!

You will need:

- Three flowerpots
- Three sunflower seeds
- Some soil
- Some water
- A dark cupboard

1 Plant three sunflower seeds in some soil. Water them and wait for them to grow. Label the pots 1, 2, and 3.

2 Put plant 1 on a sunny windowsill. Put the other two in a dark cupboard.

3 Water plants 1 and 3 when they need it. Don't water plant 2.

4 After a week, compare the three plants and write down what you see.

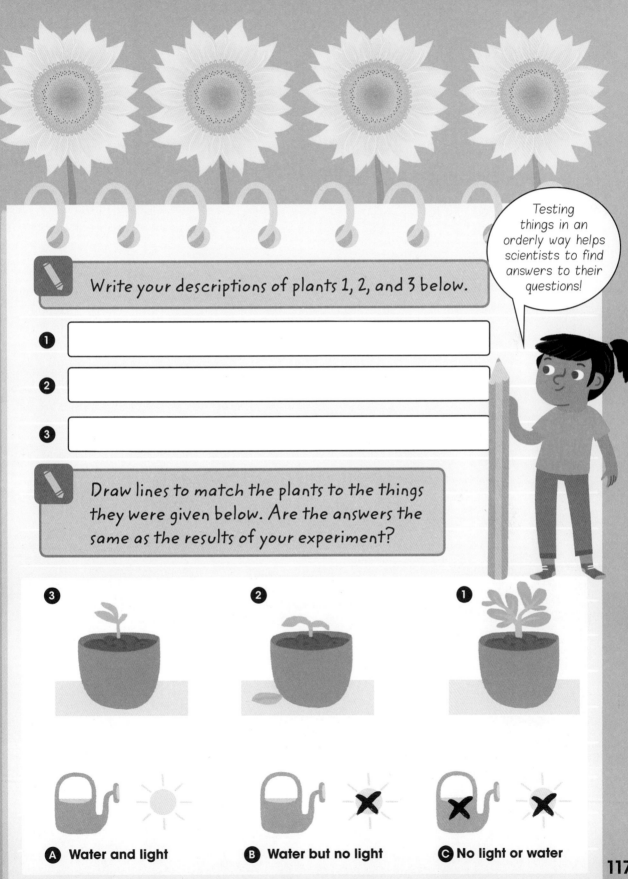

Write your descriptions of plants 1, 2, and 3 below.

1
2
3

Draw lines to match the plants to the things they were given below. Are the answers the same as the results of your experiment?

Testing things in an orderly way helps scientists to find answers to their questions!

3   2   1

A Water and light   **B** Water but no light   **C** No light or water

Fantastic fungi!

Mushrooms, toadstools, and molds are not plants or animals. They belong to a different group of living things—the fungi.

Mushrooms and toadstools grow in soil, on tree bark, or on rotting wood.

Fungi grow on the things they feed on. They take in food through a network of very thin, hairy roots.

Unlike plants, fungi don't use sunlight to make the food they need.

EXPERIMENT ZONE

The molds that grow on rotting food are actually fungi. See for yourself by growing a gross mold garden in a jar!

The yeast that is used to bake bread is also one of the fungi.

You will need:

- A old food jar with a tight lid
- Old bread and fruit
- Water

1 Sprinkle water on a slice of bread and a few pieces of fruit.

2 Put them in the jar, and then screw the lid on tightly.

3 Keep the jar for several days. Look closely, and you'll see mold starting to grow!

Don't unscrew the jar, because mold can be bad for you. When you're finished, throw it away.

Life long ago

Long ago, living things on Earth were different to those of today. Millions of years ago, amazing animals such as dinosaurs roamed our world! Scientists learn about these living things from the past by studying fossils.

Scientists who study animals and plants from millions of years ago are called paleontologists.

Animals such as dinosaurs are no longer alive because they became extinct. That means all the animals of that species died.

Fossils give us clues about how an animal lived. The fearsome teeth of *T. rex* show that it was a meat-eating dinosaur.

We know about extinct animals from their fossils.

Tyrannosaurus rex
(died out 66 million years ago)

FOSSIL NEWS

Here's just one of the ways a fossil can form. Usually only the hard parts, such as bones, are turned into fossils because the soft parts rot away.

The animal dies and its remains get buried, for example by a landslide.

Over many years, layers of mud settle on top, which get squashed down and turn into rock.

Water flowing through the rock dissolves the bones. The space fills up with minerals, forming a stony fossil skeleton.

Fossils are revealed when rocks wear away or scientists dig for them.

Dinosaur-hunting scientists dig fossils out of the rock. Color the shapes with dots to reveal this fossil skeleton.

Do aliens exist?

Scientists study life on our planet, but they also search for life on other planets. So far, they have not found any evidence of alien or extraterrestrial life, but they are still looking!

We have explored some of the planets and moons in our Solar System. Astronauts have visited the Moon, but they found no signs of life there.

Space scientists have found many planets similar to Earth. There could be life on them. But they are so far away, we can't travel to them to see.

Several robotic rovers have explored Mars. These robot vehicles work like mini science labs. They carry out tests on their surroundings and search for signs of life.

Aliens might look very different to us. Imagine and draw an extraterrestrial life form here!

Robotic rovers, such as the Curiosity rover that landed on Mars in 2012, have cameras, chemical sensors, and tools such as drills and lasers for testing the rocks on the surface.

So far, scientists have not found any signs of life, present or past, on Mars.

Glossary

Atoms The very tiny particles that make up matter.

Big Bang A huge explosion that scientists think was the start of the universe.

Chemical A material that is the same all the way through and not a mixture.

Chemical reaction This happens when two or more chemicals combine and their atoms rearrange to make new chemicals.

Circuit A loop of metal or other material that electricity can flow around.

Classify To sort something, such as living things, into different types and groups.

Combustion A scientific word for burning.

Contract To shrink or get smaller.

Crust The hard, rocky outer layer of planet Earth.

Density How heavy something is for its size, depending on how tightly the matter in it is packed.

Echo A sound that has bounced off of a hard surface and can be heard again.

Echolocation A system that animals, such as bats and dolphins, use to sense objects by bouncing sounds off of them.

Energy The power to do work or make things happen.

Evaporate To change from a liquid into a gas.

Expand To enlarge or get bigger.

Extinct If a species is extinct, it has completely died out and no longer exists.

Extraterrestrial From beyond planet Earth.

Fossils Remains or marks left in rock by living things that died a long time ago.

Friction A dragging force that makes things slow down or grip when they push or rub against each other.

Fungi A group or kingdom of living things that includes mushrooms, toadstools, and molds.

Galaxy A huge cluster of millions or billions of stars.

Gravity A force that makes objects pull toward each other. Earth's gravity pulls people toward it.

Kingdom One of the main groups of living things, such as plants, animals, and fungi.

Latin An ancient language used by scientists to give names to living things.

Life cycle The sequence of changes a species of living thing goes through as it is born, grows up, and has babies.

Magma Hot, molten rock found inside planet Earth.

Materials The different types of matter or stuff that things can be made from.

Matter The stuff that makes up all the things, objects, substances, and materials in the universe.

Minerals Natural solid substances found on or in Earth's crust, such as gold, salt, and quartz.

Orbit To move around a star or planet in a circle or ellipse. The path an orbiting object moves along is also an orbit.

Prism A triangular glass shape used for refracting light.

Properties The things that materials can do that makes them useful in different ways, such as being strong, bendy, or see-through.

Radio waves A type of invisible wave that can be used to send signals long distances.

Reflection The way light or sound can bounce off of a surface and travel in a new direction.

Refraction The way light bends as it moves from one see-through material into another.

Solar system The Sun and the planets, moons, and other objects that orbit around it.

Species The name of a particular type of living thing.

Spectrum A range of different colors or types of light.

States of matter The forms that materials can exist in, such as solids, liquids, and gases.

Surface tension A pulling force that makes the surface of water behave as if it has a "skin."

Theory An idea scientists have that explains how something works or why something is the way it is.

Universe Space and everything in it, including all the stars, planets, objects, and other matter.

Vibrations Quick, repeated movements backward and forward.

Water cycle The sequence of water evaporating into the air, forming clouds, and falling back to the ground as rain.

Water vapor Water in the form of a gas.

X-rays A type of wave that can be used to photograph the insides of the body.

Index

Answers

Page 9

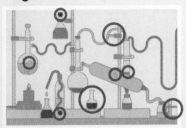

Pages 12–13

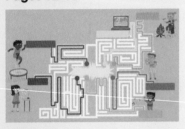

Page 16
Alice Through the Looking Glass

Page 19 A flea!

Pages 22-23

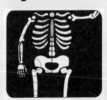

Page 31
Sound travels 1,000 ÷ 3 = 333.33 yards in 1 second, so the castle is 333.33 yards away. (The sound travels there and back as an echo in 2 seconds!)

Pages 34–35
1—B, 2—C, 3—E, 4—A, 5—D

Page 40
1—push, 2—pull, 3—pull, 4—push

Page 52
The cork, apple, and wooden ice pop stick float.

Page 61
It is 1,000,000 atoms thick!

Pages 62–63
The natural materials are paper, diamond, wool, tree bark, wood, leather, flower, cat fur, cotton, gold, and the seashell.

Page 81
The water level increases 100 milliliters, making the volume of the crown 100 cm³.

Page 85
The constellation is Ursa Major.

Page 91
3—Gold

Page 97

Pages 102–103
Animals and plants are living things. Robots are not (they can't grow, eat, or make more of themselves).

Pages 104–105
The living things are: toucan, giraffe, apple, tree, pinecone, zebra, fungi, butterfly, snake, banana, ladybug, cactus, crocodile, elephant, and whale.

Pages 106–107
2—Cat of the woods

Page 111
1—True (the skull bones of children join together as they grow up, so adults have fewer bones). 2—True (there are 206 bones in the adult body). 3—False (it's in the ear).

Page 113
There are 20 leaves.

Page 117
1—A, 2—C, 3—B

Page 121